Ghosts and syntax. These two elements help form the rhetorical spine of Kathy Goodkin's astonishing debut book as she explores what it means to be haunted. Referencing the legend that certain bridges are inhabited by ghosts of crying children, *Crybaby Bridge* is a mythic journey through humidity-drenched, insect-whirring terrains where issues of grief, stasis, desire, and textuality are probed, especially in her extraordinary sequence "Sleep Paralysis." Restless and revelatory, Goodkin's poems unfurl much like a filmstrip as her cinematic eye moves us from one striking image to the next: from "a red horse marring the field" to floodlights roaming "across the fields like lithe animals." By turns feral and ethereal, *Crybaby Bridge* will vibrate its way through your body like summer thunder.

—SIMONE MUENCH, author of *Wolf Centos*

The poems in Kathy Goodkin's *Crybaby Bridge* delight and astound! A ceiling fan is "an asterisk in a room"; tree roots are "cursive letters in a tangle." I won't look at any object again without wondering how Goodkin would see the same thing, and that is exactly what literature should do—change our perception of the world for the better.

—SHAINDEL BEERS, author of *Secure Your Own Mask*

KATHY GOODKIN

Moon City Press

MOON CITY PRESS
Department of English
Missouri State University
901 South National Avenue
Springfield, Missouri 65897

First Edition

Published by Moon City Press, Springfield, Missouri, USA, in 2019.

Library of Congress Cataloging-in-Publication Data

Goodkin, Kathy
Crybaby Bridge: Poems/Goodkin, Kathy, 1981—

2019951728

Further Library of Congress information is available upon request.

ISBN-10: 0-913785-43-0
ISBN-13: 978-0-913785-43-0

Cover illustration and interior design
by Charli Barnes
Edited by Karen Craigo

Manufactured in the United States of America.

www.mooncitypress.com

For RJ—you know where to meet me.

Thank you to everyone who has taught me, talked with me, walked with me, and supported me along the way. Most especially thanks to my family, here and departed; my generous and insightful teachers at the University of Illinois Chicago and George Mason University; my colleagues at various institutions; my children; and my friends. I'm a lucky soul.

ACKNOWLEDGMENTS

Many thanks to the editors who published versions of poems from this manuscript:

Several of these poems appeared in previous forms in the chapbook *Sleep Paralysis* (dancing girl press, 2017).

Banango Street: "Crybaby Bridge"

Denver Quarterly: "Practice Sleeping"

Dreginald: "Ancient of Days," "Ex-Portraiture, Translation," and "Why Ghosts Come Back in Clothes [One day my body was erased]"

Field: "Moving Day"

The Jet Fuel Review: "Sleep Paralysis [This nothing landscape]"

Josephine Quarterly: "Dear Extraterrestrial" and "Why Ghosts Come Back in Clothes [Tonight the domestic]"

Redivider: "Depot, Depot"

Rhino: "Michigan Nocturne" and "Pentimento"

The Volta: "Insect Poetics"

TABLE OF CONTENTS

Crybaby Bridge

SLEEP PARALYSIS

Ceiling fan an asterisk in a room

where houseplants gather weak light into masses.

Let go of the whole ensemble of *home* and *homes*,

memory of a red horse marring the field.

I wake up in a den or riverbed, dirt dregs and fur.

I wake up in a city's close syntax.

I wake up in a suburb full of other people's dinners.

Each awakening is its own ensemble.

Before you are right or wrong about something, there is just the hot vacuum of air around what you are going to say. In the interest of transparency: I call one cycle of sound *a sleeplessness*. In that insects usurp my authority. Or *cicada, cicada, cicada* (I once mistakenly labeled *locust*), which despite rumors does have a mouth in its armor. Sound depends on soundlessness; a sleeplessness is also silent. Or the desiccated lizard I found on a bridge yesterday.

In that Paul Celan writes in and of sound, beyond sense, beyond sense, through sound: *from smokemouth to smokemouth*. In that authority is not absolute, but is still located in sleeplessness: cicada, cicada, cicada. Or the dogs have chased a giant roach under my sofa.

In that insects and ghosts are the planet's most populous denizens. Sidewalk, city center, savannah, swamp, interstice. To say an insect is sibilant is false. In that insect authority is sleepless even when silent. Is chemical and crisp.

SPONTANEOUS GENERATION

I got alive
the same as you:
salt made

a small reckoning.
The night or day
crumbled and sang.

It was a kind of December
or actually December.
I wasn't there yet.

I don't know
much else about
my making.

Only I imagine
the frozen limbs
of trees touching

DEIRDRE'S LAMENT

As if a bed might hold
the answers. As if
the phantom bed
might continue to tingle and burn.
To be done in, of all things,
by beauty.

I was born with a birthmark
in the shape of Ohio
on my back.

To be born beautiful. To cast
curlers on the floor
spelling "cover me."
To scry
in the bathroom mirror. As if
the answers might swim up
from the depths
of the scratched glass.

Of blossoms:
I only ever bloomed
like an oil stain.

Of traps. Of exits: none
save the one wrought
in the skull. To be done in,
of all things, by the self,
by surviving.

As if anything could have stopped it.
    To want more than
what was given. Foretelling
    is a dangerous pastime.

PRACTICE SLEEPING

Thought I saw a man in the airport, moving through a veil of moving.
Meaningless or made from middle meanings.

Once I lay down for three whole hours. My heart was breaking.
Away outside the window, a souped-up cityscape.

Enter this breathing, this moment against movement.
I've already betrayed the city. I will not, I will NOT say "the body."

Once I had a missed connection. The whole fucking frontier
    was looking for me.

I went out every night with a black lace bra under my nightshirt.
I held the handrails of every moving walkway.

DEPOT, DEPOT

Remember when we thought we could make models, destroy them,
and the world would rip in half like a sheet of paper?

I took your name in my hand, or a train horn.

Then nothing called us on the phone.

We watched a blue-lit window on a dark back road.

In this time and place my outsides are buried (by accident) under a tree.

We lay the rest of ourselves on the floor and look up at the molding.

We watch headlights make a name on the ceiling.

We don't say it out loud, or we can't, or you do once and everything
stops ticking.

For every color I can move across the sky with one hand, ten more
won't budge.

PENTIMENTO

He has tattooed his losses
on the inside of his forearm — Lilac. Bluebell.
A season's worth of fading azaleas.

All last May, I didn't have a name
for the smell that was strung up everywhere
like rosaries. I was a blue car

stretching an asphalt canvas:
too fast to learn the language. I could not spell.
He took me, and together we lifted

the edge of a parking lot. Underneath,
tree roots like cursive letters
in a tangle. I traced the lines, each to each.

They were scaly and brown, the thickness
of our fingers. Somewhere in this story
there were two girls named Anna,

and I wound up alone,
chalking words on my lintel,
my lexicon translucent as a streetlamp.

MOVING DAY

They're threading the creek
through a tube, red clay on red clay

where grass was stripped away.
They're making the creek a secret,

hiding it beneath a place they'll call
White Pine Hills or White Oak Harbor

or White White Acres.
I like that the creek is still there.

I love its movement under me
like I love plate tectonics, the whole planet

eating and making itself from itself.
I like that it slows them,

stalls their stripping, tree ripping,
makes them touch something

that moves a world, grain by grain.
I hate that everything's for sale,

even the field fires, the thin veil
of smoke drawn over the trees.

STRIP

Even a bunch of balloons
outside Party City
is a miracle on Tuesday.

Tuesday, a head of cauliflower.
Tuesday, a discount mattress store.

Just let out its blood
and the body stops—
big bad body.
What a poser.

Haunting is a hold,
another kind of coveting.

What I would give
for a beer right now,
anything to keep
the clouds in place.

Please, can you stop them
from scraping
like bleached-white teeth
across the sky?

ELEGY

Not silent, no.
News streams

through every channel:
creek, gutter, TV screen

in neighbor's window,
the engines of passing cars.

The dead, clothed in treetops,
speak with the authority of treetops.

Every pocket sings
in tongues. Trumpets sound

from front yard magnolias,
from leaves veined like a river delta.

Controlled by nothing,
owing nothing, tall grass

on the highway's edge
would take a scythe.

Too long to mow.
Foxtail makes words

that disappear
as it grows.

REVOLUTION

After he taught me to peel carrots with a butter knife,
he sang a song about Baphomet.
We were in his dark car.
I called him Goya, but he didn't care.
We got married the next day.
It's not as serious as it sounds.
The wind was a clown, and the moon
moved on roller skates. Now I think of him

often as the mountains pull night down
and the foothills crowd like geese.
He left a fistful of bills on the bar with his keys.
When I woke in the car, the sky turned
like a wheel. The grass was gone
and the engine was running.

ABILENE, KANSAS

Russian olive leaves are silver
in the dark. Behind trees, the land rises
like a body under blankets.

I stole a chicken and killed it.

I walked down Third Street, lit
by the lights of a laundromat,
passed an ADULT sign,

two abandoned gas stations.
I was headed for the crease
where we always meet.

It was spring. I was hungry.

In the darkness
on the edge of town turbines reeled
the clouds across the sky.

DOLORES

I

Waking to salt words on the floor,
a walking stick pointed at a small black
book,

I rode out on horseback at dawn.

II

Death is always ten minutes early—
death on a fencepost, timing time.

I went to the kitchen for the soup bones my mother left.

III

He spat like an animal.
We joined him, animals
around a mound of broken glass.

We beat the walls with our hands.

The curtains my mother had sewn lay in shreds.

SATURN RETURN

I. BACK TO BLACK

As skin fills the frame
like ink in water—
not an emblem, not a mood

not a gesture
or practice pigment
but a planet of emergency—

the body lies motionless. The body
that just last night
was on the phone. Let's step back

from the picture, the lurid frame
fading into the future.
Let's start again. *The body*

is always someone's
beloved. The body
on the bed named

in the newspaper,
pulled from the Seine,
stitched into itself,

thinly held.

II. BLACK EYED DOG

At the door
to my stomach,
strings vibrate.

Bile rises.
I can hear your ghost
and you're not dead

yet. That's what
you do. Your dead
voice issues from

the body. The body
who can still say its name,
still stretch its long legs

before rising.

III. SHADOWS AND LIGHT

A cutting voice
clears the fiber
of the room,

sorts us
into before and after.
The body is

not there
anymore.
How banal: grief is gone,

now this is you
on melancholy.
Look how it rewrites

your light-filled
frame, the skin
you danced in.

No one can agree
on the source
of your pain.

Feathers spring
from your mouth
without sound.

TETRAGRAMMATON

I kept the stolen voice in a soda can.

I put the soda can in the shed.

The shed's window lit up at night,

like someone was welding inside.

When I took the can out of its hiding place

behind the lawnmower, it was heavy,

much heavier than a jar full of sand.

Forget it, forget it. But I said it out loud.

SLEEP PARALYSIS

The best time of day was watching airplanes come down from the bright or overcast or midnight sky. I was usually warm in a dress he bought me.

Sometimes on the early side, sometimes a little later than that, the floodlights moved out across the fields like lithe animals. One swept by me and went away in the shape of a dog I once knew.

WHY GHOSTS COME BACK IN CLOTHES

No one really owns anything,
despite the radio's assertions.

Do you remember the radio?
What a thing.

The night I moved in
to my new house

a shade in the doorway
said *Where is Marie.*

In my dark bedroom
I told him *Not here.*

All I've seen is some land
on the edge of town

where the houses appear as insects
from a great height.

No one can own them.
In the dry city, pigeons

delineate the bleachy light.
There are a lot of things

that aren't buildings,
and you can't own them, either.

Even the promise of rain,
I told him, *is a truer story.*

CINÉMA VÉRITÉ

When a car is pulled from the river, we know this future is just to the west of another future, where the car rolled backward over the bridge and into town. In a hail of delicate stay-tabs, in a rain of gravel and ants, a car plunged into the river at a single point. The point moved outward, a clock on the surface of the water. The bartender refuses to serve a future that lingers around town; the other futures defect and come sadly in like refugees, and a car is pulled from the river at noon. Sheet metal and glass are added together, added up. They equal what happens; for example, the river drips in pieces from the eastern side of a car. When a day is so hot that dust from the road coats the skin, the crooked future bends back. Here it comes with a fistful of facts.

NIAGARA FALLS

Can you see it, she asks, holding the fat girl
up to a window. Fat girl dangles like a pair of dice

from a rearview mirror. Mom is not fat,
but her hair is formless, her striped tank-top stained

with interlocking brown rings. An overflowing plastic cup
of Sanka was a stencil on her belly as she lay in the motel bed

for a very long time last night. Fat girl peeled the paper wrappers
off all soaps in the bathroom and poured a tiny bottle of shampoo

into the toilet. Bubbles in the current, a film
of foam. At the Falls, everyone puts on

a funny paper hat. Looking out of the scratched plastic,
they watch water pile itself on itself.

SLEEP PARALYSIS

Even if you named a gas station mini-mart after me,
I still wouldn't love you.

The burnt sidewalk eyes me like any other Tuesday.
In old photographs, you stare past the camera.

People mix in the street but keep their own shapes.
I take the shape of whomever I touch.

Ventriloquist radio in the distance,
brainless chatter in a junkyard.

Outmoded oracle.

CRYBABY BRIDGE

I

Clouds low over a new city

Not new-to-me newly citied

glassed and upright crane's arm a fixture

Watch the skyline layer up like a body

in real time

cells dividing and dying

II

Strung out on support beams

hung highest in a bad world the villain

I take pictures but I don't like pictures

Whatever sounds rise from the paved-over river

will catch the cars that cross

The engine is a fake-out these days a poor place-holding
vibration

Plants grow up through it

III

Enough already   highway

coughing in the backseat

Pull up my hood   story me into a different place

THE LAST MAN WHO SPAT ON THE FLOOR

I never heard the sound he made.

Like feet in a train station

a three-fingered hand taps the glass.

A telegraph.

Get off and keep walking.

The sign says to yield.

Why call me?

Why string me out   *here:*

twenty paces past the potter's field.

It shouldn't be

the way the story is told.

It shouldn't be my name

breaking into a room

from the cold mouth

of an archway.

EREBUS

The dogs stood on the road

or beside the road

First a black-and-white dog eyes yellow as an owl's

on the road's shoulder—

what does the road shoulder—

in the flat white light the nowhere light

sudden as if a trapdoor opened

and the dog stepped through

Then a brown dog with a torn ear

or one ear only

yes just one ear

and a gray dog with fur like crushed velvet

The next dog was huge, with a lion's mane

The next was whippet-thin

white with pink eyes

They lined the road and we walked

no, we drove at the speed of walking

moving through their ranks   a single-car parade

The air smelled of swamp gas

You had your hand on my hand

or on my thigh

These dogs mean there must be people nearby

you said   I know where we are

That was clearly a lie

All the dogs watched silent

moving only their eyes

THE WANDERING JEW

There is always room to be surprised,
I read in a women's magazine.
It wasn't my magazine.
I was reading over a stranger's shoulder.
She ignored me, or else she didn't notice.
She turned the pages at regular intervals.
We sat in an airport, back to back in the attached rows of chairs.
She was behind me so I twisted around to look behind me.
We both read her magazine for some time.
I looked at the window beyond her;
on the runway, it was raining.
In the glossy glass, on the woman's black sweatshirt,
I saw the unmistakable shape of Mickey Mouse.
Mickey Mouse makes me sadder than perfume.
Nothing and no one should make such promises.
The woman kept turning the pages in her magazine.
I turned around and settled into my seat,
but sometimes I turned around again
to look out the window at the runway where it was raining.
The runway was empty. The flight was delayed.

SLEEP PARALYSIS

This nothing landscape pulls last night's dreams
from my head like strings of beads.

Rocking chair, mocking bird.

Where have I heard it before?

My attention to detail wavers.

I can't think a thought without the word *getaway* or the word
caught.

Bats in the basement maintenance room;
I saw them through a window in the parking lot.

Some spice in the air, like a small explosion.

Something happened to your car.

There was a brown overcoat and a crowbar.

Nothing lasts forever, and even so.

Nothing feels as good as always not having you.

ANCIENT OF DAYS

When I was a city, I was a horse.
I could cry at anyone's home movies.
Bruised haircuts, inflatable pools—
I would score them all in B minor.

I saw the end of me on a baseball diamond.
One hand was on my crotch, the other in the sky.
I punched the air. It wasn't sad,
it was triumphant, me dust-covered and dying.

After that, the screens were lit, the reels all rolling.
I rode out along the highways into the stadium night.

It is the end times and also a time of sandwiches. I didn't know sandwiches would still be a thing. I didn't know I would still wear jewelry and complain about waiting in line, would walk through a graveyard finding patterns in dates, names, ask strangers for the time, while above the clouds boil like milk. It is the end times and still there are sugar packets and individually portioned everythings: potato chips, disposable razors, mimosas in cans. A valet named Carl who is going to night school for Psychology. I didn't think the world's end would have valets, or night classes, or Psychology. Once, I wrote a poem about the world's end, how it happened when Europeans invaded Africa, the Americas, Asia, et al. And how it kept happening, kept ending. Even now. Then I wrote a poem about the sky rolling up like a scroll, an image I stole. Now I'm watching the clouds cook up new words for you. It's the end times and all our bills are due.

THE LEGEND OF SOMEBODY SOMEBODY

In a hill town
I first saw his face

on the floor.
Wait, I know

how it sounds:
it was painted there

with nothing
to body itself home at night.

Then I remember there's nobody here.
Nobody shuffling cards.

A mask, an axe;
we all saw her collapse.

Sometimes I drink
until my face

skips town, walks out
along the highway.

I'll find him. We'll talk.
His is my favorite of all

the outmoded names
for darkness.

EREBUS

They spill from gaps
between floorboards, teeth,

collodion dark
where matter isn't.

Arrest me, officer,
hurry up please it's time

calls the shade in the stairway
with a clock of lead.

One promise to the dead:
your candles, decanters,

Christmas wreaths, guns
will be entombed in a $60 storage unit.

On the surface of the Earth,
Odysseus on the street

in his nightgown of skin
howls for his mom.

WHY GHOSTS COME BACK IN CLOTHES

Tonight the domestic
pretends to be the world

soft blue me-ghost riding
the sofa until dawn.

Window me this:
what moved across the room

in the early glare?
I never saw fabric like that

a part of the air.
Is it sad

all my dead lined up
behind the curtain waiting?

JAMAIS VU

Every situation holds hostages

event with its own horizon

I watch the prairie sky become itself

my mind a record needle

on the roadside caught

a skip where a white dog appears

No punchline here:

I forget what

season

I should have these feelings in

Could be the season of

watery light

Could be the season of limestone

Everything is liquid

in the road

Even my own thoughts circumscribed

PSALM

On a night you could catch something from
        (gnats in columns, noise from a parking-lot carnival)
a man in a vest with no shirt underneath
        drifted down the highway embankment.
He spoke like a black-headed goat
        and everyone in the area code became hungry.
Look at the strings of headlights, trucks, and bicycles.
        Little white Christmas lights.
Music piped in from the sky or some nearby gas station.
        Reflections in the water-filled ditch reaching toward their
origins.
What he said was that blue isn't a color.
        What he said was an empty stomach.
Amazing, after that, there are still sheets to wash and string up.
        Even the telephone lines are beautiful hatchmarks
against a cloudless, colorless sky.
        He said where the ferry crossed the river
he placed bright gulls and ships.
        They were years in the making:
mechanical bulls dismantled, gears repurposed,
        and the men working on boats were so like men
until they fell as though seized by sleep.

Half-light tombs a city
too humid to ever hurry up.
What they fought over
(a topiary, sex, the last time,
the time before)
we'll never know.
As for the disposition
of her physical remains—
hurry up please it's time.
The dead are stacked
like books on a shelf.
It's time, past time
to move somewhere else.

WHY GHOSTS COME BACK IN CLOTHES

Why should I find
a background beautiful
through a camera?

Why means *where*
when I pass the old markers
of your passing.

In pictures, you never appear
where you should,
slow silver pooling

around your absence.
I'm beside everything:
myself; the point.

Just pull the last threads
from September. Wind them
around me while I sleep.

Show me
your hands
in my dreams,

like they're real
human hands
full of blood.

EX-PORTRAITURE (TRANSLATION)

Take a picture of me with this cat

who is not my cat but my brother's cat,

and has the nose and eyes of a man.

The balcony floor is littered;

I sweep, leave all doors unchained.

Waiting for your entrance I read old text messages,

which I saved and will continue to save.

My hand is a ham when I hold it to the camera.

My hand is bigger than the cat.

My broom is made from light, the cousin of nothing.

Light is straw or like straw.

SLEEP PARALYSIS

I am often too scared to look. When I hear
a whistle, a picnic bench or pair of pants
come to mind. But then a dog might appear,
and pull behind it, like a filmstrip,
a many-framed lit-windowed train.
Look, there I am behind a freight yard,
with my face to a fence watching
an empty boxcar. Or a bridge at night,
cars' headlamps like will-o'-the-wisps, ghosts
of light, crossing. I bow my head.
Whatever is already in eyeshot is *of* me,
but not those things that lurk
behind the hedges of my brows. Every day
when I walk to get eggs or milk
the woods along the street are full of figures.
I know them. They stand between the trees.
I cannot see them but I know them. I know what they want.

OBJECT PERMANENCE

"… a child will point to a part of the horizon where nothing is moving and tell the mother that a man is coming."

How can I carry
the ribs of a piano?
The measurable sun
is in ribbons on the floor.

Tear away the wrapper.
Destroy the object
that I might hold
its memory close.

I saw feet
beneath my closet door.
I saw a man
with the head of a boar.

I heard your mother's voice
but she had not survived,
saw a white cat sitting
at the end of the drive.

A house full of no one,
our instruments
dressed in wood, singing
We'll never get out of this world alive.

AFTER HOURS

A town full of dentists closes at sundown.

Everyone goes home to turn on the lights.

Then they all wander into the winter clothes

they folded and stashed under their beds last night.

Over the back-handed carpet, feet slide and step,

but the floor whispers *stay* under its frictiony breath.

I used to think pictures were all I had left,

until I found this minute, and the next.

How can a lamp measure loss?

It's a barometer, a mean matter-of-fact barmaid.

Woodchips and mint call me out

to the space behind the neighbors' garage.

OK, religion might live here: a gravel patch at midnight.

No frame can reconcile this feeling. No picture can save us.

LANDSCAPE WITH 4-BEDROOM BRICK RANCH AND TYPOLOGY

Some days I hate it. I hate it
as I hate sleep, how it numbs the edges
of the pine trees, arborvitae,
scalloped lawns, drooping blue hydrangeas.

Still, people die here too, sometimes
strung up like Christmas lights
in the garage, or shot
in their driveways by police.

Despite a fleet
of neighborhood planners,
these streets delineate
neither safety nor autonomy,

and the drowned always return,
hair-first, triumphant
as swamp grass rising
from the reservoir.

Yes, I hate it. And
if I weren't here,
I wouldn't be me,
the only refuge I know there to be.

PAUL BUNYAN APPROACHES

All our TVs, computers, phones
short out with the first lightning strike.

Just TVs, computers, and phones;
the house lights stay lit.

We wait and watch
the windows for news.

It's not hail that whitely rides
the storm like static.

It's not feathers or debris.
Something else, like light

on the finest airborne matter.
A dusting of snow or ash.

NEBRASKA BOUTS-RIMÉS DIPTYCH

I

A house in every town is burdened
with hardwood footsteps tapping
carpeted stairs. They'll say the cat brings
those dead birds to the door. It first occurred
to the neighbor when, from a vacant house, he heard
a spoken word. Or those birds flapped in-
to the glass, an accident, bird blood mapping
their slide to the grass. Yes, the blurred
figure in the window, palm pressed to pane, can't
be anything. Just reflections. No collar
of memory could be buttoned around
a smell, contain shuffling dance-
steps and tinny phonograph. There's fodder
here for foxtail. Scrap metal for foundry.

II

The radio's ongoing burdens
are percussion and bass. The tapping
of fingers. Trapdoors on springs
open to hair steeped in smoke. It occurs
when you lift the hinges of the parking lot: herds
of bison spill out, skin like sails flapping
around thin frames. Chase the crows off your map: in
high relief, grass. Then speed and building outlines blur.
The barn running alongside the car cants
back and whispers to the culvert. A dog collar,
flotsam rides the runoff, kite-strings wrap around
horsetail, golf balls do-si-do. A dance
band is playing on the radio, fodder
for your invitation to the lost and found.

WISTERIA SINENSIS

The bus stops at the river.
There's nowhere else
I'd rather be.

Good thing I love your dead.
I love them
more than my own dead,

how they telescope
out of you
when you speak.

I love the powdery blue
of them, the sudden smoke.
Some days I think

I'll let them take me.
The river's grown-over
margin is a sanctuary.

Sometimes it's a tomb.
I can't always tell the difference
between the two.

SEX POEM

Your ribs
shot through
with barn weeds
and thistle,

you sing to me.
Cars sweat sun
in the driveway nearby.
We hear them

through the heat,
through your close,
rusty song.
Your thighs matted

with bottle glass
and beetles,
you sing to me:
song of paper scraps,

song of roof tiles
fallen to the ground.
Cars in the field, cars
in the yard, cars

on the highway break
into your song,
carry it with them
until you're gone.

WHY GHOSTS COME BACK IN CLOTHES

One day my body
was erased by crows
cawing in the background
on TV.

I watched
the screen
as decades
unfolded.

In America, ghosts
never show up naked.
They wear
English dresses,

Italian lace,
Revolutionary War uniforms,
Civil War uniforms,
World War I uniforms,

Iraq War uniforms.
Are these
my only options
or limestone?

When a child
first appeared
next to me, nude
and pellucid,

I named it.
I called him Him,
and taught him words
by singing them.

No matter how many crows I count
there's always one more
caught in the branches.

Meaning: I misread
the street sign "Topsail"
as "Horsetail"

and preferred my misreading.

DEAR EXTRATERRESTRIAL

Why does the sidewalk just sit there
while the stars alphabet the sky?

It is everything. I thought it would be.
Which is to say I am disappointed.

So please describe these objects in orbit:
an Indiana farmhouse, a closet full of skirts.

Whether they are "skirts" or "a skirt" I cannot discern,
but the torn edges flap and gingham is on the breeze.

Now here you might see more light,
writing the basest of stories: asphalt,

old potpourri charm, flies wings, &c.
individually packaged against dust,

alphabetized in bulk bins.
The applications are so many,

a great number of mites on my hands.
This is the conclusion. Bye. I said *goodbye*.

I am due to watch a man pace on a fire escape,
and very soon the TV light will break my carapace.

like bodies
will be unmade
like the forest
unmakes me

I lie in the leaves
and the bugs
are safe inside me
are at home

inside me
in the nest
of my body
the wet grass

of my body
my ears and eyes
shelter them
vines climb my body

men who walk
over me
cannot see
my body

they can see
only bodies
like mirrors
bodies that

will also be unmade
but now are glossed
bright as quarters
and my body is not a body

for them
is a forest
body, a body for
bugs, vines, fungus

the godhead fungus
that lives
in all bodies
that is my body

the way my blood
was my body
my respiration
and perspiration

but I don't assume
any other aspects
I am not anything
else, I am my body

and the bugs
and vines and spores
are my body
and it's OK to look

now, look
at my unmade body
look at me

PUNNETT SQUARE

On a bus, I'm faster than the weather.
I count over two hundred deer beside the highway.
I have a headache and it's you

in my ear again, whispering
barley. Or maybe you said *rye*.
How many kinds of grain can you name

with your hand down my shirt? Don't talk
to me about fields until you understand
the word *pastoral*. No one meant you

to look like you; your face is nature's accident.
You've never seen me eat.
I'll put grass seed in your gas tank.

I'll beat my clothes against the rocks.
I'll bathe at the edge of the river I once saw
reflected in the windshield of your car.

MATRYOSHKA DOLL

The soil was like skin
underfoot. Walking
was an exercise
in intimacy.

Later that summer,
thick with bagworms,
I bore a child.

My body's aloneness
nested in summer's aloneness,

my body's thundering
in summer's thundering.

MICHIGAN NOCTURNE

All those unseen parts
under the hood. Don't touch
anything. Your car,
all ravel and rust
might collapse, unsung

in some junkyard.
Let evening (replete
with barking dogs)
flirt with the windshield,
strum that unstrung guitar

while it quietly pries
off your hubcaps. Mold
wet mud stars around a string

of broken light bulbs.
Hang them on the tin fence
to dry, then swing
them round and round,
hurl them into the sky.
Like old horror movie
blood, your car's oil on the dull

dirt of the driveway runs toward the street.
What could I do
but put my hand
in the space between
the car's front seats?

Great trucks slouch over the highway
to I don't know where.

I move at the speed of my mind,
or maybe a second delayed.

My vehicle arrives just after an accident.

A second is a funny genre.

Cosmic joke; little echo.

A second is the cousin of now
like light is the cousin of nothing.

Light has no genre;
light has all genres.

Either way, it always beats me to the scene.

PESACH AUGURY

Twisted bark on the ground
turns into dead bird
and back to itself again,

a long way to travel
for small carbon.
I walk the garden path

until night falls,
percussive. The air
is red with city clouds.

I wear it like a coat.
I can't stop thinking
about a single mulberry

on the doorstep
this morning,
smeared like old blood

from a sacrifice—
but no mulberries
for months now.

Sacrifice is fraught.
It's the wrong word
for what happens

when someone is killed.
No one is sacrificed
to shooters, police,

or systems
as jealous as God.
It's like *holocaust*:

as if we placed them
on the altar like Isaac,
so many rams, caught.

Hurry up please,
it's past time
to find new words

for those taken,
pushed down
the dry steep hillsides

of death, reduced
to carbon, poured
from the glass,

turned into a night sky
red and full of ash.

ELEUSINIAN PARAPHRASE

I'm walking in the woods with my two-year-old and thinking about the story of Persephone. It's fucked up. Persephone's child-rapist uncle abducts her and takes her to the underworld basement where he lives. When her mother, Demeter, begs Persephone's father to help rescue her, he says, *Well hold on there honey, there are two sides to the story*. Persephone's father is the king of the gods. I'd sooner trust a spider. My own daughter is a streak of color through the woods, a half-thought too fast for words. Real spiders can see music, shape webs to sounds we can't perceive. The woods are full of them. On past a constellation of mushrooms on a fallen tree: *Water, water*, my child cries. Not from thirst; from delight and surprise. Some spiders give their bodies to their children, are consumed by them, give up their guise. That's nothing I know about. But I do mother more than my mind, moving after her, just behind my eyes.

IDEAS ABOUT THE THING

Idling engine,
the ending of summer.
The air leafed and flaring

messaged me,
arrived as my steps
sounded. As though

it came from my mind,
the sun was a note
in the conducting air.

I texted everyone I knew.
I was in a state
when the rain reached in

and pulled out a cry.
It seemed as though
it came from outside.

SLEEP PARALYSIS

None of the signs in this rest stop point the way out.

The picnic tables are all nailed down.

It might have been snow in that field,

or else it was water reflecting the clouds.

Under a drop-ceiling sky,

my mind a ball bouncing along the ground.

Dun birds fly from silos at dusk—no, that's a different place.

Past a one-way sign in the middle of a lake.

NOTES

In urban legend, a crybaby bridge is a bridge from which one can hear a ghost child or children crying. There are crybaby bridges all over the U.S. Some folklorists have disputed the claim that crybaby bridges are legitimate folklore and believe that the stories were created more recently and spread online.

Sleep paralysis is a condition that causes a person to experience temporary physical paralysis upon waking, and is sometimes accompanied by hallucinations.

"Insect Poetics" borrows a phrase from the Paul Celan poem [Landscape with urn beings], as translated by John Felstiner in *Selected Poems and Prose of Paul Celan.*

"Deirdre's Lament" alludes to events in the story of Deirdre of the Sorrows, a prominent figure in Irish mythology.

"Depot, Depot" takes its title from the Tom Waits song of same name.

"Abilene, Kansas" borrows the phrase "darkness on the edge of town" from Bruce Springsteen's song/album of same name

"Dolores" borrows images and phrases from the story "Florencita and El Zorillo" in *New Mexico Ghost Stories* by Antonio Garcez.

"Saturn Return" takes the names of section titles from albums/a song: the album *Back to Black* by Amy Winehouse, the song "Black Eyed Dog" by Nick Drake, and the album *Shadows and Light* by Joni Mitchell.

"Cinéma Vérité" takes its title from a method/style of filmmaking, primarily used in documentaries.

"The Last Man Who Spat on the Floor" takes its title and some images from a story by the same name in *Ghosts, Ghouls, and Goblins of Colorado* by Maryjoy Martin.

"Erebus" [The dogs stood on the road] borrows some syntax from Brigit Pegeen Kelly's poem "Dead Doe." "Erebus" is a figure/concept/place from Greek myth, generally understood as the essence of darkness and/or the place where the dead go before proceeding to the underworld.

"The Wandering Jew" takes its title from a pervasive (and varied) myth about a Jew who is doomed to wander the Earth until Jesus' return.

"Ancient of Days" is a biblical name for God, sometimes in mystical Judaism meant to connote the very source of God, a sort of proto-God, or the aspect of God that is eternal.

Lines in "Apocalypse Whenever" allude to Revelation 6:14, "The sky vanished like a scroll rolling itself up, and every mountain and island was removed from its place" (*The Harper Collins Study Bible*, New Revised Standard Version, 1989).

"Erebus" [They spill from gaps] makes reference to a scene in *The Odyssey*, Book 11, in which Odysseus enters the kingdom of the dead and learns of his mother's death by the presence of her spirit there.

"Jamais Vu" is a condition in which a person knows that they have previously encountered something but feels as though they're encountering it for the first time. It's more or less the opposite déjà vu.

"Psalm" borrows its final phrase from Robert Pinsky's translation of *Inferno*.

"Louisiana, Year-and-a-Day" takes its title from a New Orleans burial practice. According to an interview with a local cemetery director published in *The Haunting of Louisiana* by Barbara Sillery, bodies may be removed from the grave one year after burial in order to make room for new bodies. The remains are sometimes kept in pouches in a storage room, or sometimes disposed of. The poem also borrows some phrases from the story "The Madam Who Won't Lie Still," also published in *The Haunting of Louisiana.*

"Object Permanence" takes its epigraph from an article, "Attachment Behavior Out of Doors," by J.W. Anderson, collected in *Ethological Studies of Child Behaviour* (ed. N. Blurton Jones, 1972). The poem's final line is taken from the Hank Williams song "I'll Never Get Out of This World Alive."

"The Geography of Nowhere" takes its title from a book by James Kunstler: *The Geography of Nowhere: The Rise and Decline of America's Man-Made Landscape.*

"Made Things" is written after the Sally Mann photographs *Body Farm* and includes a few lines from Walt Whitman's *Song of Myself.*

Lines in "Pesach Augury" refer to the story of Abraham and Isaac, Genesis 22 (*The Harper Collins Study Bible*, New Revised Standard Version, 1989); the phrase "the dry steep hillsides of death" is borrowed from Ursula LeGuin's *A Wizard of Earthsea.*

"Eleusinian Paraphrase" refers to the story of Persephone's abduction by Hades, as told in Ovid's *Metamorphoses*, translated by Charles Martin.

"Ideas About the Thing" borrows syntax and form from the Wallace Stevens poem "Not Ideas About the Thing but the Thing Itself."

CPSIA information can be obtained
at www.ICGtesting.com
Printed in the USA
FFHW021856301019
55888829-61760FF

9 780913 785430